The Swot Book of Animal Biology

Helen Veeder

A step-by-step guide to the basic facts you need to know to help you get to the top of the class in Animal Biology

D1927870

Wolfe

First published 1975 by Wolfe Publishing Ltd.,
10 Earlham Street, London WC2H 9BR

©1975 Wolfe Publishing Ltd.

SBN 7234 0484 4

Set in 11/13 Journal by
Cold Composition Ltd., Tunbridge Wells, Kent.

Printed by Williamsons, Worcester Park, Surrey.

ABDOMEN

The part of the body of a mammal posterior to the diaphragm containing the liver, kidneys, etc. In insects it is the group of segments behind the thorax.

ADAPTATION

Changes in the inherited characteristics of a living organism over a long period of time, which tend to improve the chances of survival of the species. (See *Evolution.*)

ADAPTATION TO ENVIRONMENT

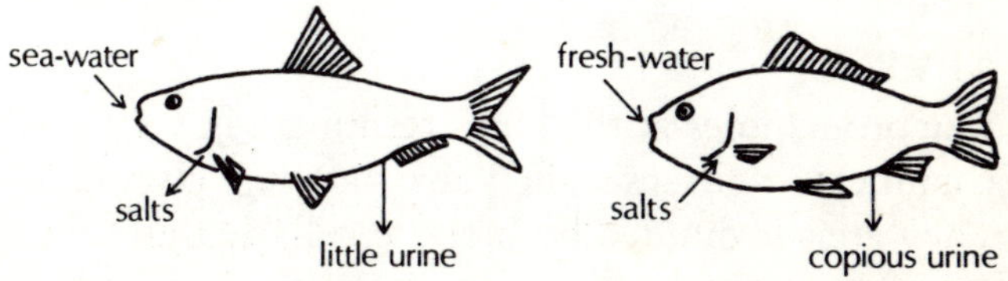

MARINE FISH FRESHWATER FISH

ALIMENTARY CANAL

The gut. The system in the body concerned with the intake, digestion, and absorption of food, and the final elimination of unwanted material.

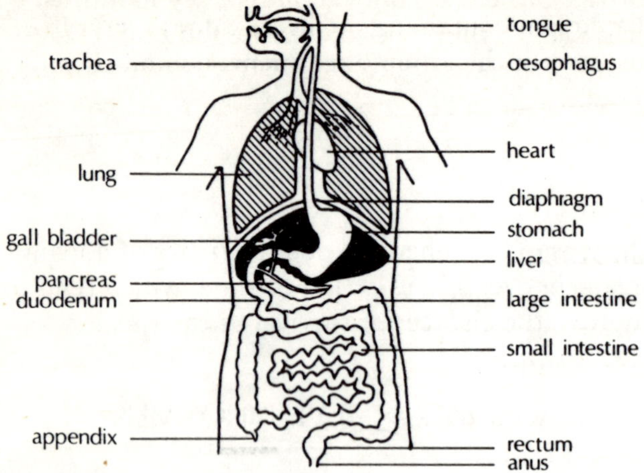

ALVEOLI

The bronchioles in the lungs terminate in very small chambers or airsacs, called alveoli, (*sing.* alveolus). They are surrounded by blood capillaries, and the gas exchanges take place across the single-celled layer between.

AMINO ACID

Chemical compounds, all with the same basic structure. They all contain nitrogen as well as carbon, hydrogen, and oxygen, and some contain sulphur. Although there are only about twenty identified amino acids, they can combine together in chains in such a variety of ways that a very large number of proteins can be formed, many of them containing large numbers of amino acids.

AMOEBA

Unicellular animal living in fresh water. It is of no definite shape as it is constantly changing in movement.

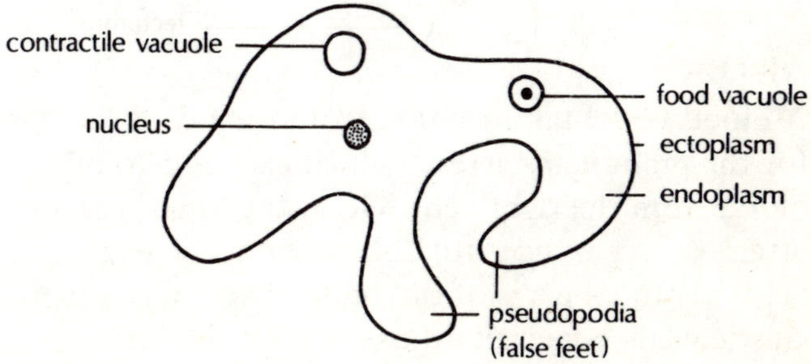

ANAEROBIC

Describes organisms that live without using free oxygen to obtain energy from the breakdown of food. *Example*: yeast.

ANTIBODIES

Chemicals produced in the blood as a defence against specific infection. Their presence in the blood confers immunity against subsequent attacks.

ARCHAEOPTERYX

A fossil showing characteristics of both a reptile and a bird, thereby providing the first evidence of the evolution of birds from reptiles. It has a bird-like beak, but reptilian teeth, and both feathers and claws on its wings.

ARTERY

A blood vessel taking blood from the heart. Except for the pulmonary artery, which carries de-oxygenated blood from the right ventricle to the lungs, the arteries carry oxygenated blood from the left ventricle to all parts of the body. They have tough elastic walls, especially those nearest the heart where the pressure is greatest. Unlike veins, they have no valves.

BACTERIA

Very simple microscopic organisms of various shapes,

usually regarded as belonging to the plant kingdom. They multiply quickly, and are found everywhere. They are of very great importance. Some are beneficial to man, for example, in the soil, and in antibiotics. Others cause diseases.

BILE
A fluid made in the liver which breaks down fats and oils to make their digestion easier.

BLOOD
A fluid found in animals which carries materials in special vessels to all parts of the body.

Composition of Human Blood

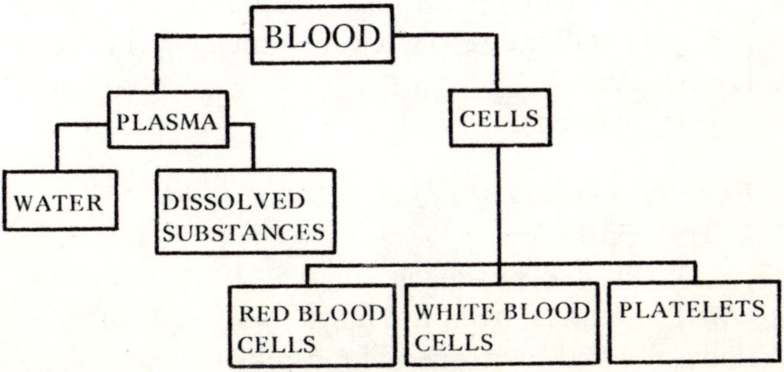

1. Plasma

Consisting of

(a) water

(b) dissolved substances:

salts, mostly sodium chloride

glucose, amino acids, fats — products of digestion

hormones

enzymes

urea, dissolved carbon dioxide — waste

2. Cells

Consisting of

(a) red blood corpuscles: approx. 5 million per cubic millimetre

(b) white blood corpuscles: approx. 7 thousand per cubic millimetre. Two kinds: phagocytes and lymphocytes

(c) platelets.

Functions (Uses) of Blood

1. Transportation

(a) Products of digestion

(b) Oxygen, from the lungs to all parts of the body. Carried by the red blood cells.

(c) Waste products
(d) Hormones, antigens, etc.

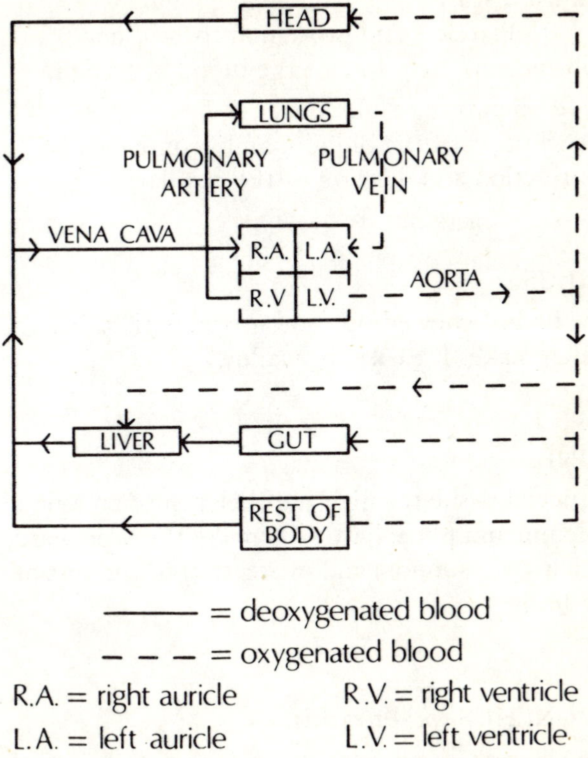

BLOOD CIRCULATION (DIAGRAMMATIC)

2. Protection

(a) White blood cells, (leucocytes). Protection against disease.

(b) Platelets and protein in the plasma, (fibrinogen), help to clot the blood if needed.

3. Temperature regulation

Distribution of the blood mainly controlled by contraction and dilation of the capillaries.

BOLUS

The ball of chewed up food mixed with saliva which makes it easier to swallow.

BONE

A special tissue forming the skeleton of an animal. Calcium and phosphate salts make the bone hard which gives support and protection to the rest of the body.

BRONCHUS (*pl.* bronchi)

Air passages or tubes connecting the trachea to the lungs. By branching and dividing they lead into the very small bronchioles.

BRONTOSAURUS

Giant reptiles, living about 150 million years ago. They were plant eaters, and measured about 70 feet long.

CALORIE

A unit of measurement for the energy value of food. For example, one gramme of carbohydrate can provide 4.0 kilocalories of energy.
1 kilocalorie = 4.2 kilojoules.

CAPILLARIES

Extremely small blood vessels through which oxygen, carbon dioxide, glucose, amino acids etc, can permeate into or out from the cells.

CARBOHYDRATE

Energy-giving foods containing carbon, hydrogen and oxygen. *Examples*: starch (in potatoes, bread), sugar.

CARNIVORES

Flesh-eating mammals, usually referring to vertebrates. *Examples:* lion, fox, shark.

CARTILAGE

Tissue similar to bone, but tough and flexible. It is found at joints, and often acts as a shock absorber.

CELL

A single unit of living material.

Living organisms are made of cells which are themselves composed of chemical compounds.

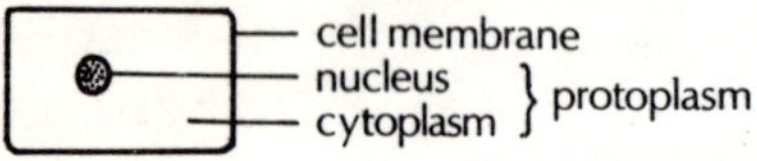

ANIMAL CELL (DIAGRAMMATIC)

RED BLOOD CELLS

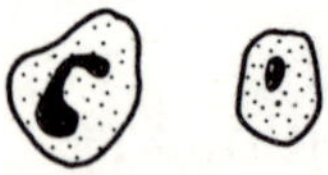

WHITE BLOOD CELLS

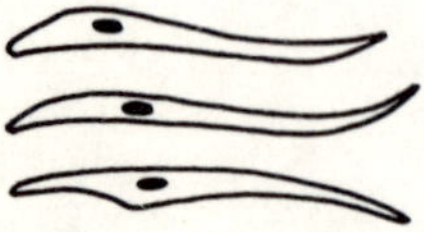

SMOOTH MUSCLE CELLS

EPITHELIAL CELLS WITH CILIA

ATOMS

↓

MOLECULES

(chemical compounds)

↓

CELLS

↓

TISSUES

↓

ORGANS AND SYSTEMS

↓

LIVING ORGANISMS

Helpful Units and Relative Sizes

1 millimetre (mm)	= 1000 micrometres (μm)
1 micrometre	= 1000 nanometres (nm)
Unicellular organisms	= 1 mm
Eggs (ova)	= 1 mm to 0.1 mm
Approx. limit of unaided vision	= 0.01 mm
Cells	= 0.1 mm to 1 micrometre

Bacteria	= 1 micrometre
Limit for light microscope	= 0.1 micrometre
Viruses and very large molecules	= 0.1 to 0.01 micrometre
Molecules	= 0.01 micrometre to 1 nanometre
Atoms	= 0.1 to 0.001 nanometre

CHROMOSOMES

Thread-like matter found in pairs in the nucleus of a cell. They consist of long chains of complex chemical compounds, and are concerned with reproduction and inherited characteristics.

Number of chromosomes in man: 46, (23 pairs).

CHYME

The semi-liquid mixture of food and gastric juices present in the stomach during the digestion of food.

CILIA

Microscopic hairs which move rhythmically. In

some cases they propel the whole organism, in others they help to waft the material along the surface of the tube or duct. *Examples:* cilia are present in the lining of the respiratory tract, to prevent dust, etc., entering the lungs. Cilia are present in filter feeders like molluscs. They help to waft the food into the animal. Cilia are found in unicellular animals as aids to movement in water.

CLASSIFICATION OF ANIMALS

A. INVERTEBRATES (animals without backbones):

Protozoa: unicellular microscopic animals. Many are parasitic and cause disease. *Examples:* amoeba, malarial parasite.

Porifera: very simple many-celled animals. They live in water and do not move, obtaining food by water flowing in and out of the many openings. *Examples:* sponges.

Coelenterates: they consist of two layers of cells, forming a tubular body with a single opening, usually surrounded by tentacles. In coral a hard calcareous exoskeleton forms. *Examples:* hydra, jelly-fish, sea-anemone.

Platyhelminthes (flatworms): worms with flattened bodies. Most are parasites. *Examples:* tape-worms, liver-flukes.

Nematodes (round worms): unsegmented worms with round bodies. Some are found in the soil, while others are parasites. *Examples:* hookworm.
Annelids (segmented worms): segmented worms with round bodies, often bearing bristles. *Examples:* earthworm, ragworm, leeches.
Molluscs: soft-bodied animals with a muscular foot and usually having single or double shell, often coiled. They are mostly aquatic. *Examples:* snails, mussels, octopi.
Echinoderms: Marine animals having radial symmetry. They are fairly immobile but have sucker-like feet, and tubes through which water circulates. *Examples:* star-fish, sea-urchin.

ECHINODERMS: SHOWING RADIAL SYMMETRY

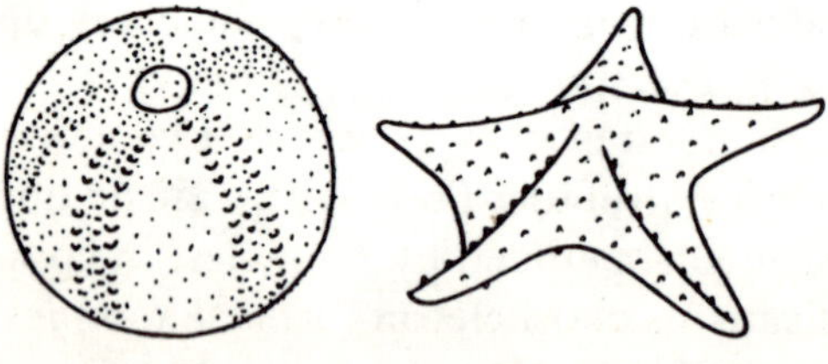

Arthropods: a very large phylum (group), which includes several classes. They are segmented, with jointed limbs, and an exoskeleton (skeleton outside the soft parts of the body).

(a) Crustaceans: most are aquatic and breathe by gills. They have several pairs of limbs and antennae. *Examples*: crabs, shrimps, woodlice.

(b) Insects: there exist very large numbers and kinds. Their bodies are divided into three segments, with three pairs of legs, and usually two pairs of wings. *Examples:* ant, bee, fly, butterfly, locust.

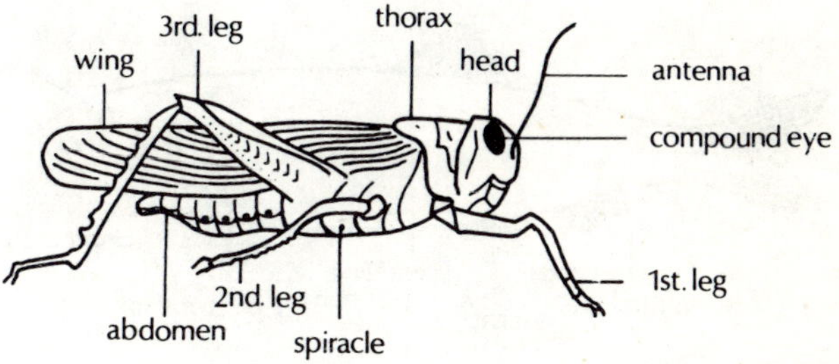

LOCUST

(c) Myriapods: their long bodies are divided into very many segments, with one or two pairs of legs to each segment. *Examples:* centipedes, millipedes.

(d) Arachnids: the body is divided into two parts, and they have four pairs of legs. *Example:* spiders.

B. VERTEBRATES (animals with backbones, and typically two pairs of limbs, but these may show considerable adaptation to a particular mode of life, and in some cases the limbs may not be obvious or developed, for example, in the snake, whale and seal):

(a) Fish: these live in water and breathe by means of gills. They have a scaly skin, and fins. They are 'cold-blooded', and usually lay eggs which are fertilised externally. *Examples:* cod, salmon, pike.

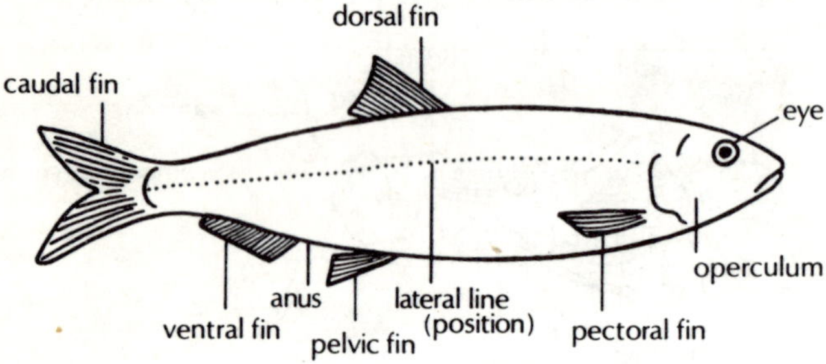

FISH: a herring

(b) Amphibians: They begin life in water, breathing by means of gills, as seen in the tadpole, but as adults they develop lungs and live partly or wholly on land. They have four limbs, no scales on their skin, which is usually moist, and lay eggs which are fertilised externally. They are 'cold-blooded', *Examples:* frog, newt.

(c) Reptiles: they have scales on their skin, and

limbs with claws. They lay eggs with leathery shells on land, though many live in or near water. Snakes are without limbs, though vestiges are seen in the skeleton. They are 'cold-blooded'. *Examples:* snake, lizard, crocodile, tortoise.

(d) Birds: their skin is covered with feathers, and the fore-limbs are adapted for flying. They are 'warm-blooded', and lay eggs, which are hard-shelled. They usually exhibit considerable parental care. *Examples:* swallow, eagle, duck, penguin.

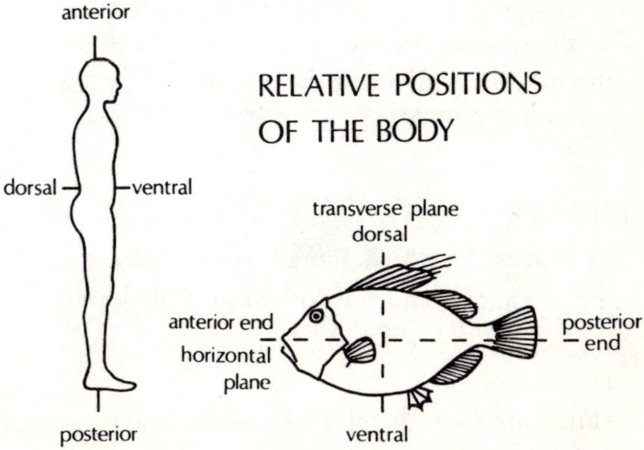

(e) Mammals: they are 'warm-blooded', with hair on their skin. They suckle their young with milk, from mammary glands. They are, in general, intelligent and adaptable. *Examples:* man, deer, elephant, mouse, lion, bat, whale.

CYTOPLASM
The clear jelly-like material of the cell, excluding the nucleus, which contains various structures not usually visible. Many chemical reactions concerned with living processes take place here.

DIAPHRAGM
Muscular tissue dividing the abdomen from the thorax in mammals.

DIGESTION
The process by which animals break down their food so that it can be absorbed into the blood. (See *Alimentary Canal.*)

Final products are glucose, amino acids, glycerol and fatty acids.

They are absorbed through the walls of the small intestine.

Human Digestion

FOOD TYPE	REGION	SECRETION	ENZYMES	BREAKDOWN
CARBO-HYDRATES	Mouth	Saliva	Ptyalin	Starch to maltose.
	Duodenum	Pancreatic juice	Amylase	Starch to maltose.
	Small intestine	Intestinal juice	Sucrase	Sucrose to glucose.
			Maltase	Maltose to glucose.
			Lactase	Lactose to glucose.
PROTEINS	Stomach	Gastric juice	Pepsin	Proteins to poly-peptides.
	Duodenum	Pancreatic juice	Trypsin	Proteins to poly-peptides and amino acids.
	Small Intestine	Intestinal juice	Peptidases	Poly-peptides to amino acids.
FATS	Duodenum	Pancreatic juice	Lipase	Fats to fatty acids and glycerol.

DINOSAUR
Term describing a variety of reptiles which lived about two hundred million years ago. The age of reptiles lasted about 150 million years (Mesozoic era).

D.N.A.
Initials representing deoxyribosenucleic acid, a very complex compound found in the chromosomes of all living things, forming the genetic material.

DORMANT
An organism existing in a sleeping, or inactive state.

EAR

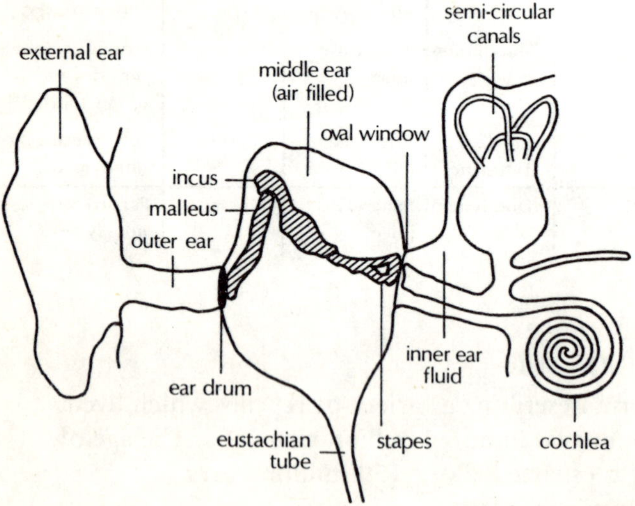

ECOLOGY
Study of the relationships between plants and animals and their environment.

EGG (see *Yolk*)

EMBRYO
The animal developing from the fertilised egg, before hatching or birth.

ENVIRONMENT
A characteristic place or area in which an animal lives, including the conditions of temperature, light, etc.

ENZYMES
A protein found in small quantities in living organisms which controls the rate of important chemical reactions without itself being changed. There are many different kinds, each with its own special purpose. *Examples:* the name of an enzyme often indicates the substance it acts upon, as in maltase, (acts upon maltose), or it may indicate the type of reaction, as in oxidase, (oxidation).

EPITHELIUM
A type of tissue consisting of layers of cells,

sometimes only one single layer of cells. It is found on both the outer and inner surfaces of the body, and its function is mainly protection. *Examples:* found lining the respiratory tract, and the intestine.

EVOLUTION

A natural process by which there is a gradual change in the characteristics of an organism over a very long period of successive generations.

Evolutionary Time Scale

PERIOD	MILLION YEARS AGO	ANIMALS FIRST APPEARING (approx).
Cambrian	500–600	Invertebrates
Silurian	350	Fish
Devonian	300	Amphibians
Carboniferous	250	Reptiles
Jurassic	180	Mammals, birds
		(Man)

'The age of reptiles': 230–70 million years ago.
'The age of mammals': 70 million years to the present day.

EXCRETION

The removal of waste products from the chemical processes of the body in a living organism. *Examples:* via the kidneys as urine, the skin as sweat, and the lungs as carbon dioxide and water vapour.

EYE

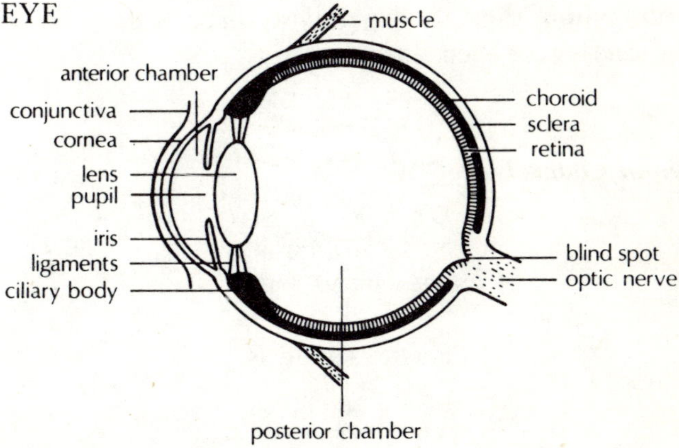

FAT

Energy-giving food. An organic compound containing carbon, hydrogen and oxygen. When stored in the body of animals it acts as an insulating layer under the skin, and as a food reserve. *Examples:* butter, suet, margarine.

FERTILISATION

The joining of male and female parent cells to form the new cell which will develop into the new organism.

FOOD CHAIN

The link between widely different organisms, but upon whom they are dependant, directly or indirectly, for their nutrition.

Food Chains

ENERGY FROM THE SUN

↓

PHOTOSYNTHESIS

↓

GREEN PLANTS
(energy producer)

↓

HERBIVORES
(primary consumer)

↓

CARNIVORES
(secondary consumer)

Examples:

(a) grass ⟶ cow ⟶ man.

(b) plankton ⟶ small fish ⟶ large fish ⟶ man.

(c) green vegetation ⟶ deer ⟶ lion.

(d) grass ⟶ cow (cheese) ⟶ mouse ⟶ cat.

FOSSIL

The remains of an animal or plant that lived thousands or millions of years ago. They are usually hardened by deposits of mineral salts, or seen only as traces on a rock.

GENE

Units of the chromosome in the cell which decide inherited characteristics.

GENETICS

The study of heredity: the inherited characteristics of organisms and their variations.

GILLS

Organs of respiration in fish and some other aquatic

animals. Fine filaments, (rich in blood vessels), provide a large surface area over which water is drawn, and where gaseous exchange occurs.

GLANDS
Organs of the body, each of which produces for various purposes different and important fluids which, in the case of the ductless glands, are transported round the body by the blood. *Examples:* salivary glands secrete saliva, mammary glands secrete milk, and endocrine glands secrete hormones.

GLUCOSE
A sugar. Made by plants in photosynthesis, and an important product of digestion in animals. A source of energy. (See *Carbohydrates.*)

GUT
Tube through which food is taken in and digested. (See *Alimentary Canal.*)

HABITAT
A characteristic place or area in which an animal

lives. *Examples:* sea-shore, heathland, marsh.

HAEMOGLOBIN
A protein present in the red blood cells. It contains iron and is responsible for carrying oxygen all over the body from the lungs. It is bright red when oxygenated, and blue-red when deoxygenated. This is the reason for the difference in colour between the blood of arteries and veins.

HEART
A muscular organ which acts as a pump driving blood round the body.

HERBIVORE
An animal that only eats plants. *Examples:* cow, sheep, giraffe.

HIBERNATION
Winter period of sleep or rest for many animals during which their metabolic rate is lowered, and the body temperature of mammals drops. Some animals awake from time to time to feed. *Examples:* hedgehog, bat, tortoise, brown bear.

HOMOIOTHERMIC

'Warm-blooded'. Describes an animal that maintains a constant body temperature above its normal surroundings. (See *Poikilothermic.*)

HORMONES

Substances which enter the blood in very small quantities from the ductless glands of the endocrine system. They affect different systems of the body, usually at some distance from the glands producing the hormone. *Examples:* thyroxine, adrenalin.

HYBRID

Offspring of parents that are genetically unalike, but are sufficiently similar for breeding to be possible.

IDENTICAL TWINS

Twins formed as the result of the division of a single egg. They are always of the same sex, and they possess identical genetic material.

ILEUM

The part of the small intestine after the duodenum.

It is responsible for the absorption of the products of digestion.

IMAGO
The final stage in the metamorphosis of an insect. It is the adult, sexually mature, form.

INSECT
A class of arthropods. They are very numerous and include the butterfly, locust, flies, and beetles. They have a body divided into three parts, with three pairs of legs, and usually two pairs of wings.

INSTAR
The name given to a developing insect, between each moult. Similar to a nymph. In the locust there are five instars before the insect is fully mature.

IRRITABILITY
The ability of a living organism to respond to a stimulus. The stimulus can be of very many

different kinds, such as light, or temperature changes, touch, smell, etc. It is an important characteristic of all living things.

JOINT

The joining of bones of the skeleton, usually designed to permit movement. Joints are also present in the exoskeletons of the insect and other arthropods.

BALL AND SOCKET JOINT

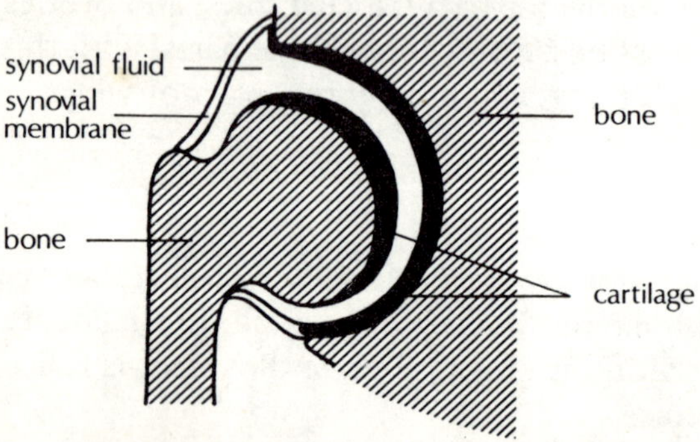

JOULE

A unit of energy. It has replaced the calorie as the unit for measuring energy obtained from foods. (One kilocalorie = 4.2 kilojoules.)

Energy value of nutrients (approx.)

	kcal/g	kJ/g
Carbohydrate	4	16
Fat	9	36
Protein	4.25	17

KIDNEY

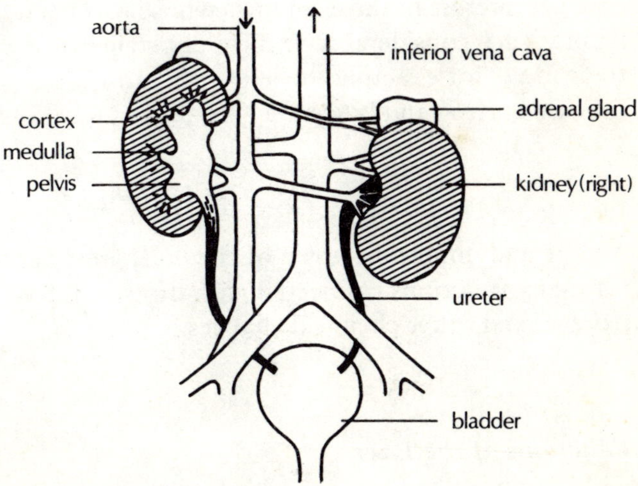

Organs present in vertebrates. They are responsible for filtering from the blood unwanted products of metabolism such as urea, and mineral salts, which are then excreted by the bladder as urine. They also help to regulate the quantity of water present in the body.

LIFE-CYCLE

The changes and development of an organism from the fertilized egg to maturity and death. It is of especial interest in those animals whose form and habitat vary considerably at different stages of their life – for example the jelly-fish, mosquito, liver-fluke, frog and butterfly. (see pages 36 and 37).

LIVER

A large and important organ of the body, responsible for many functions connected with digestion, food storage, and other chemical changes.

Functions of the Liver

1. Storing excess sugar as glycogen.
2. Breaking down unwanted proteins. The amino acids are converted to glycogen, and the part of the

molecule containing nitrogen is excreted by the kidneys as urea (in urine).
3. Producing bile in the gall-bladder.
4. Breaking down old red blood corpuscles. Some parts are excreted as urea, but the iron of the haemoglobin is stored for further use.
5. Destroying the toxic (poisonous) materials brought by the blood.
6. Helping to regulate body temperature. The large volume of blood normally present in the liver conserves body heat.
7. Controlling the level of concentration of chemicals circulating in the blood.

LIVING THINGS

Characteristics of Living Things

Movement
Excretion
Respiration
Reproduction
Irritability
Nutrition
Growth

Initial letters spell 'Merring'

LIFE-CYCLE OF FROG

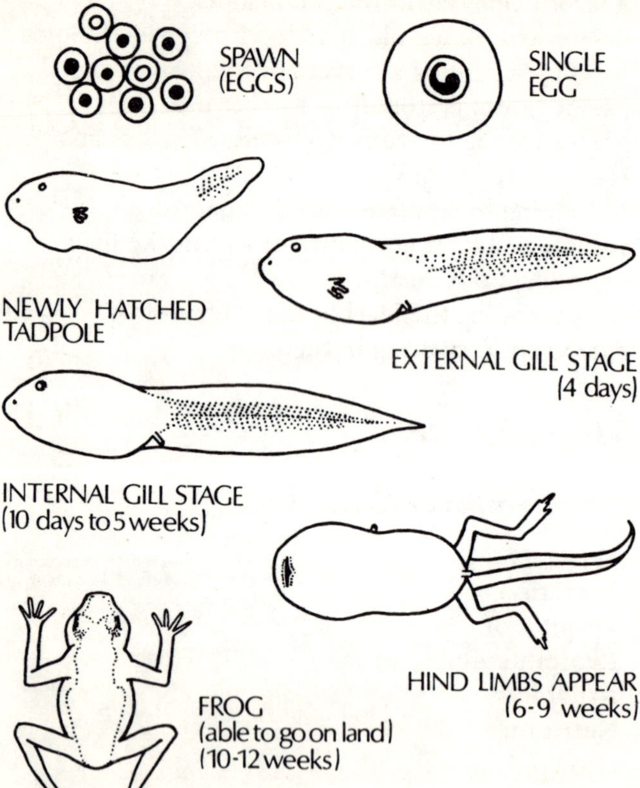

LIFE CYCLE OF THE LARGE WHITE BUTTERFLY

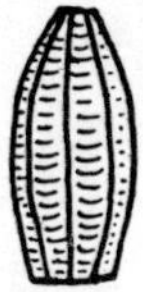

EGG

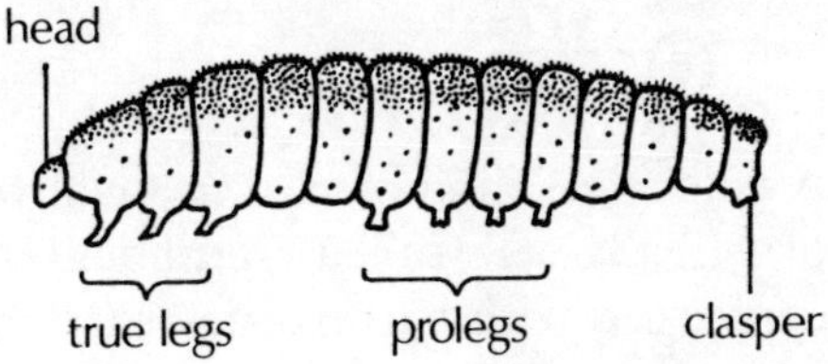

CATERPILLAR (LARVA)

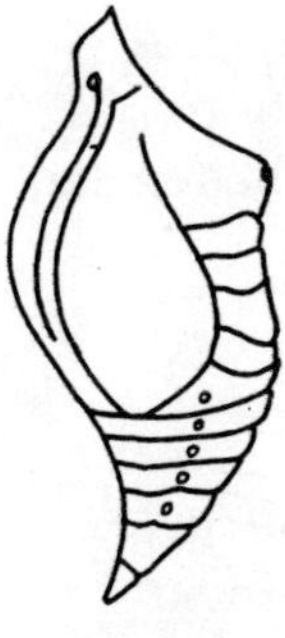

PUPA

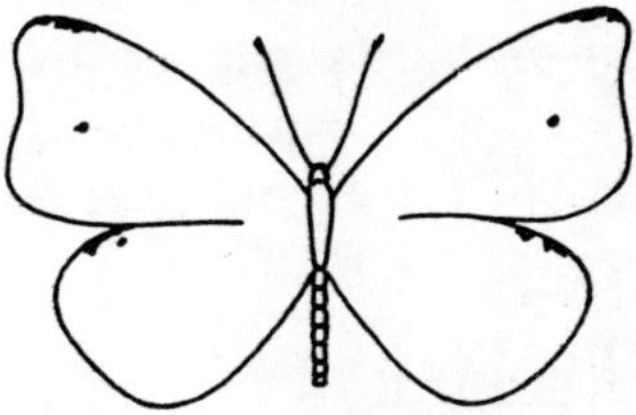

ADULT BUTTERFLY
(IMAGO)

LUNG
Important organ of respiration, where gaseous exchanges take place. (Oxygen is taken into the blood and carbon dioxide is removed.) Present

in all vertebrates except fish, where in some cases it has evolved as a swim-bladder.

LYMPH
A colourless fluid carried in small vessels. Contains principally cells called lymphocytes which are concerned with bacteria destruction.

MAMMAL
The class of vertebrates which includes man. A distinguishing characteristic is their ability to secrete milk (from mammary glands of the female), with which the young are fed.

MARSUPIAL
Mammals found mainly in Australia (some in N. and S. America). When born the young are not fully developed, and stay in the mother's special pouch where they are suckled. *Examples:* kangaroo, wallaby, opossum.

MENSTRUAL CYCLE
The events, in a monthly cycle, taking place in the

female reproductive organs, to prepare for the possible fertilisation of an ovum, and the events that follow (pregnancy, birth, lactation). Menstruation is the monthly discharge, including blood, when fertilisation has not occurred. It is caused by the breakdown of the uterine wall. These changes are largely brought about by hormones.

METABOLIC RATE

The rate at which energy is used up in the body. This varies considerably from time to time, depending upon activity, age, sex, and health.

METABOLISM

The chemical processes taking place in the living animal resulting in energy changes. (see page 40).

METAMORPHOSIS

A change of appearance that takes place in stages in the development of certain animals from egg to adult. *Example:* egg ⟶ larva (caterpillar) ⟶ pupa (chrysalis) ⟶ adult butterfly. (See *Life-cycle.*)

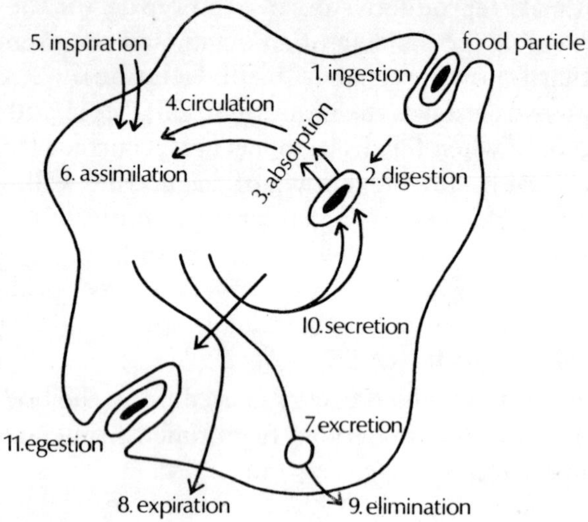

METABOLISM ILLUSTRATED DIAGRAMMATICALLY IN THE AMOEBA

MICROBE

A general term for all microscopic organisms, plant or animal. It often refers to those causing disease.

MICRO-ORGANISM

Very small living organisms, plant or animal, usually too small to be seen except under the microscope.

MUCUS
Thick, sticky fluid found in mucous membrane of vertebrates. In, for example, the respiratory tract. Also used to describe any sticky fluid or slime found in invertebrates.

MUSCLE
Fibrous tissue concerned with movement, which is brought about by the contraction of the muscle cells.

MUTATION
Changes occurring in the genes and chromosomes. These changes occur naturally, but they may also be brought about by radio-activity. They may result in the appearance of an individual markedly different from the rest of the species (a mutant). This difference may be beneficial, but it is more likely to be a disadvantage. Haemophilia and sickle-cell anaemia are the result of mutation.

NATURAL SELECTION
Members of the same species tend to show small variations in their characteristics. If these

variations are an advantage in the struggle and competition for existence, then these individuals will tend to survive and reproduce. If the variation is genetic, then the succeeding generations will inherit these differences and the advantages that they confer. Where variations are not an advantage individuals possessing them are less likely to survive or reproduce, and the variety may die out. Charles Darwin called this process 'natural selection'.

NERVOUS SYSTEM (Central nervous system)
The arrangement of nerves, spinal cord and brain in vertebrates. Sensory nerves send messages from the sense organs (eyes, ears, etc), to the brain. Motor nerves cause muscular contractions. The system in invertebrates is simpler.

The involuntary nervous system is concerned with the automatic activities of the body – such as the beating of the heart, contractions of the alimentary canal, or of blood vessels.

A reflex action: A particular type of unconscious nervous response which does not involve the brain. The sensory nerve endings transmit the message to the spinal cord which in turn sends an impulse direct to the appropriate motor nerves. *Examples:* touching a very hot object results in immediate withdrawal of the hand. A very bright light (the stimulus), causes contraction of the eye (the response). A tap on the knee causes it to jerk (caused by contraction of muscles).

A NERVE SHOWING TRANSVERSE SECTION

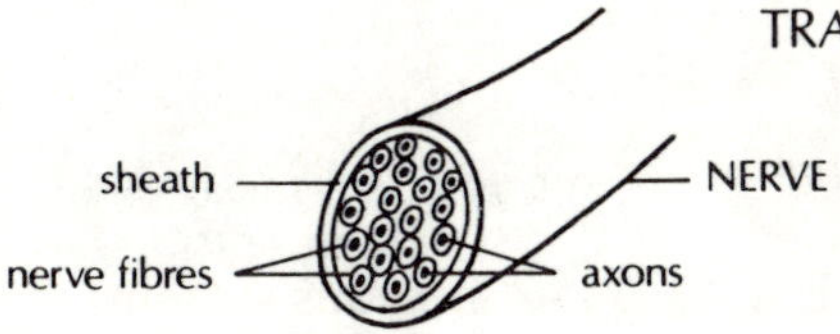

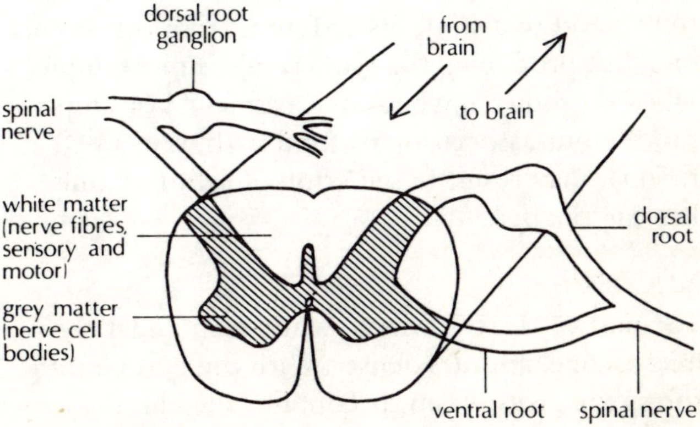

SPINAL CORD

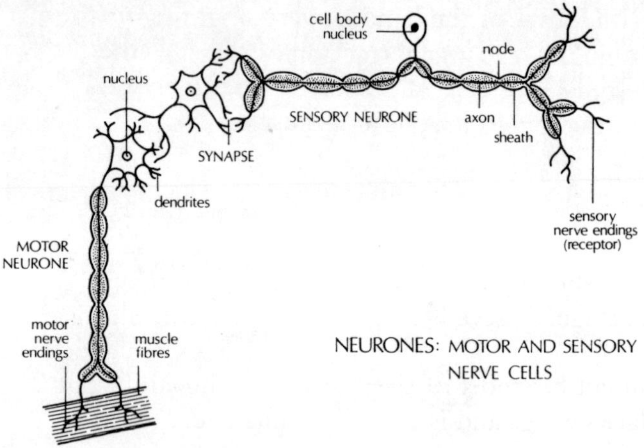

NEURONES: MOTOR AND SENSORY NERVE CELLS

A conditioned reflex: the subject may be trained to respond to a stimulus different from the original one, but producing the same result. For example, saliva is produced when food is smelled (a simple reflex), but association of food with, say, a bell ringing, may result in secretion of saliva on only hearing the bell.

NUCLEUS

The part of the cell which, when seen under the microscope, appears denser. With the cytoplasm it forms the protoplasm. It contains the chromosomes and is necessary for growth and reproduction of the organism.

NUTRIENTS
The parts of food useful to the organism. *Examples:* carbohydrates, proteins and fats.

NUTRITION
The science of food, and its use by a living organism.

NYMPH
A stage, or several stages in the metamorphosis of certain insects, for example, the locust, in which the insect has most of the features of the adult, but lacks wings and is sexually immature. Moulting occurs between each stage.

OMNIVORE
An animal that eats both meat (other animals), and plants. *Example:* man.

ORGAN
A particular part of the body, with a special function. *Examples:* heart, liver, kidney.

ORGANISM
Refers to the whole animal or plant.

OSMOSIS

The movement of water through a semi-permeable membrane (for example, cell membranes), from a dilute solution to a more concentrated solution. This controls movement of water in a living organism.

OVIPOSITOR

The tube down which an insect lays its eggs.

OVULATION

The discharge of the egg from the ovary.

OVUM

The female germ-cell, or gamete, which, when fertilised by the male gamete, or sperm, will form the zygote, from which the new individual is formed.

OXYHAEMOGLOBIN (See *Haemoglobin*)

PALATE

The roof of the mouth of vertebrates.

PARASITE

An animal or plant which lives in or on another living organism, from which it gets its food. *Examples:* tape-worm, fleas, malarial parasite.

PERISTALSIS

Rhythmical movements of the gut which push contents along.

pH

A scale from 1-14 of acidity or alkalinity. pH7 is neutral, less than 7 is acid, and more than 7 is alkaline.

PHOTOSYNTHESIS

The process by which carbon dioxide and water are converted to oxygen and sugar by green plants, using light energy. It is of very great importance to the animal kingdom, as the food they eat is dependant upon the existence of plants. (See *Food Chain.*)

PLACENTA

The tissue, rich in blood vessels, formed on the surface of the mammalian uterus where the fertilised egg has been implanted, and through which it will receive nutrition and oxygen from the mother.

PLANKTON

Very important microscopic animals or plants which drift mostly near the surface of the sea and lakes. Food for many fish and whales.

PLASMA

The liquid part of the blood, consisting of water and many soluble substances, such as sodium chloride and other salts, glucose, amino acids, hormones, etc.

PLATELET

Small, irregularly-shaped cell fragments, found in the blood, which help to clot the blood when necessary.

POIKILOTHERMIC

'Cold-blooded'. The animal does not control its body temperature, and is therefore approximately at the temperature of its surroundings. (See *Homoiothermic.*)

PROTEIN

Chemicals made of a combination of amino acids, present in all living things. As a food they are necessary for growth and development. They are found in foods such as meat, fish, cheese and eggs.

PRIMATES

A group of mammals which have relatively large brains, and climb by grasping. *Examples:* man, ape, monkey.

PTERODACTYLS

Prehistoric reptiles adapted for flying, measuring about 16 feet from wing tip to wing tip.

PUPA (Chrysalis)

A stage in the development of certain insects, such as the butterfly, which undergo complete metamorphosis. The pupa is apparently resting after the active, feeding, larval stage, but in fact, important structural changes are taking place in preparation for the emergence of the adult insect.

RED BLOOD CELLS

Disc-shaped cells in the blood containing haemoglobin which carries oxygen to all parts of the body. They have no nuclei, and after three or four weeks are destroyed by the liver, but they are being continuously replaced by new ones made in the marrow of the long bones.

REPRODUCTION

The process by which parent organisms give rise to the next generation. *Examples:* simple division of unicellular animals, sexual reproduction by male and female parent cells.

FEMALE REPRODUCTIVE ORGANS

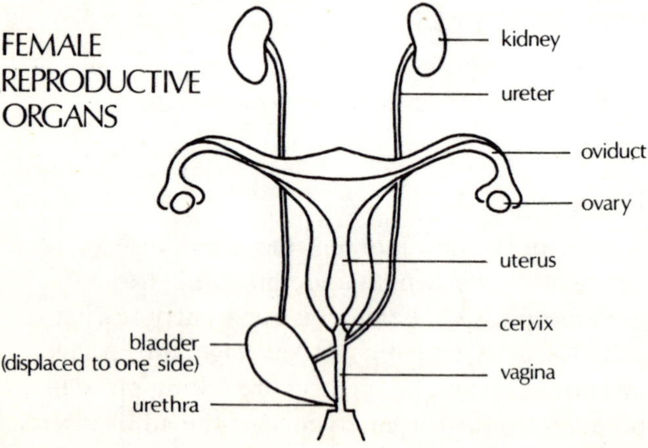

MALE REPRODUCTIVE ORGANS

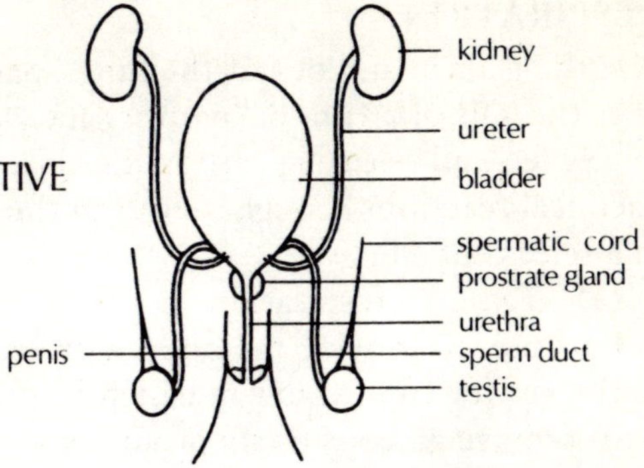

PARENT (MALE)	PARENT (FEMALE)
↓	↓
TESTES	OVARIES
↓	↓
GAMETE (SPERM)	GAMETE (OVUM)

GAMETE (SPERM) → ZYGOTE ← GAMETE (OVUM)

ZYGOTE
↓
EMBRYO
↓
FOETUS
↓
BABY
↓
ADULT

RESPIRATION

Breathing air in and out of the lungs, passing water over the gills of a fish, or by other means, taking in oxygen and releasing carbon dioxide. The chemical reactions brought about in the cells result in a release of energy.

(a) External respiration

Purpose: to provide the body with oxygen from the air, (or from water in which it is dissolved), and to remove gaseous waste products – carbon dioxide and water. Known as gaseous exchange.

Examples of methods used:

Mammals: lungs
Fish: gills
Insects: tracheae

Unicellular organisms: simple diffusion of gases through the cell walls.

(b) Internal respiration

Oxygen is required in the cells of an organism to oxidise glucose in order to release energy.

Oxygen + glucose $\longrightarrow$ carbon dioxide + water +

Energy

This takes place in several stages.

(c) Differences between air breathed in and air breathed out, in man:

	IN	OUT
Average composition of air in atmosphere		
Nitrogen	79%	Same
Oxygen	20%	16%
Carbon dioxide	0.03%	4%
Rare gases	small	same
Water vapour	varies	more than atmospheric air

The temperature of expired air is higher than inspired air – hence heat lost from the body.

(d) Anaerobic respiration

The release of energy by the incomplete breakdown of glucose without the aid of atmospheric oxygen. This occurs in the respiration of yeast, where the products are carbon dioxide and alcohol.

RODENT

A large group of gnawing mammals. They have chisel-like incisor teeth which grow continuously. *Examples:* mouse, squirrel.

RUMINANT

A group of mammals with a complicated stomach.

Food is returned to the mouth for further chewing (the cud). *Examples:* cow, deer, sheep.

SAC

A term used to describe any organ or tissue which has a bag-like shape, and can be used as a container. *Examples:* air-sac, yolk sac.

SALIVA

Digestive juice secreted from glands in the mouth. It contains an enzyme which begins the breakdown of starch to sugar, and also it helps in swallowing.

SIBLINGS

Brothers and sisters of the same father and mother.

SKELETON

The bony structure of an animal which gives support and protection. *Examples:* internal skeleton of man, external skeleton of a crab (exoskeleton).

Functions

1. It provides a strong framework, which gives support and protection.

2. It encloses and protects many important organs, for example, the brain, the spinal cord and the heart.

3. It provides anchorage for the attachment of muscles, so that movement is possible at the joints.
4. Red blood cells are made in the marrow of the long bones.

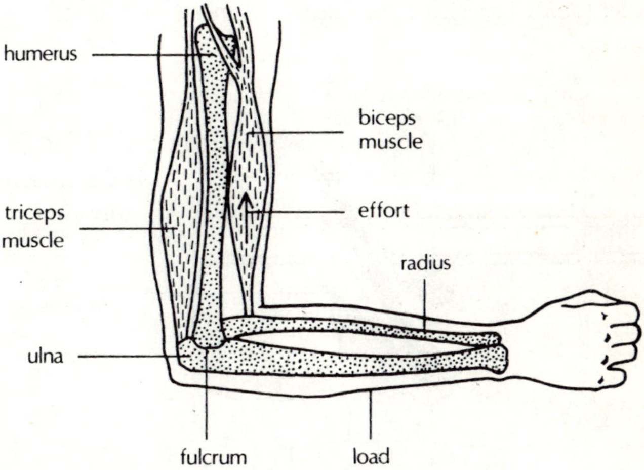

THE ARM AS A LEVER

SKIN

Functions

1. Protection of the tissues beneath from damage and infection.

2. Temperature regulation

(a) Dilation or contraction of the blood capillaries.

(b) Shivering – contraction of small muscles, which results in heat production.

(c) Sweating – glands secrete sweat on to the surface of the skin. Its evaporation cools the skin surface.

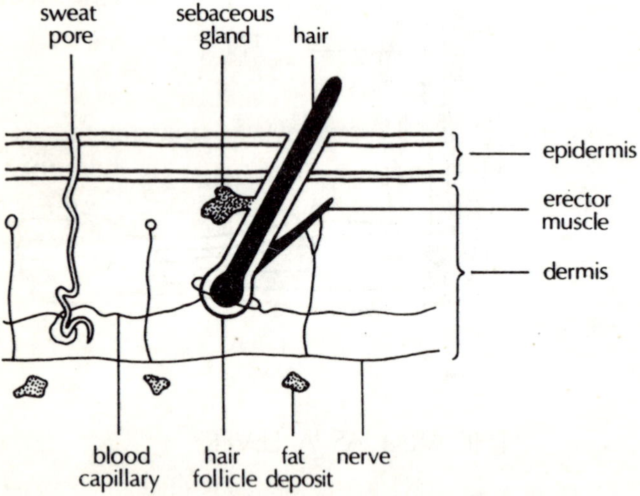

(d) Hairs (and feathers in birds), trap air, which acts as an insulator and prevents heat loss. Furry animals can increase this effect by fluffing out their fur or feathers through muscular action – an effect seen in man as 'goose-pimples'.

(e) A layer of fat helps to reduce heat loss.

3. Sensitive nerve endings makes the animal aware of touch, pain, and temperature changes.

4. Excretion: the sweat glands deposit on the surface of the skin a solution of salt, and a few other excretory substances – for example, urea.

SPECIES

Animals which are sufficiently similar to breed amongst themselves are regarded as being members of the same species. *Examples:* man, dog, salmon.

SPIRACLES

Openings down the sides of insects leading to the tracheae, which allow air to enter.

STIMULUS

Any change or disturbance which results in a response from an animal. *Examples:* A rabbit responds to the sight or smell of a fox by running away; the pupil of the eye becomes smaller if the light becomes brighter.

SWIM BLADDER

Small air bladder, present in most fish although not the shark family. The changes in the amount of air it contains alters the buoyancy of the fish, so that it can rise or sink in the water.

SYNAPSE

The space between dendrites (nerve endings), of one neurone (nerve cell), and those of another.

SYNOVIAL FLUID

Found in connective tissue called the synovial membrane. It is around joints such as the knee and shoulder. It helps to lubricate the moving surfaces.

TASTE BUDS

Nerve-endings on the tongue, sensitive to certain tastes, i.e. sweet, sour, bitter, and salt. Other flavours are in fact smelled by sensory cells in the nose.

TEETH

1. Types of teeth:
   Incisors – for cutting.
   Canine – sharp and strong, for tearing meat, and

gripping prey.

Premolar – for grinding and cutting.

Molar – for chewing and grinding – not present in milk (first) teeth.

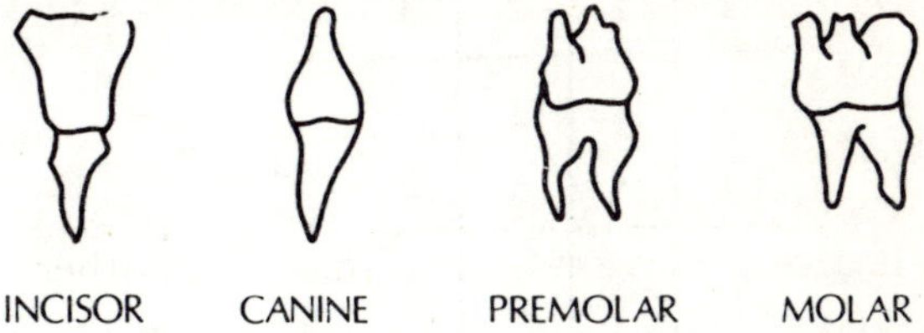

2. There is a variation in the numbers, type, and size of teeth, in different species, depending upon the diet.

Carnivores: the canine teeth are powerful and sharp, often curved. The molars and premolars are also large, and in some cases, act as shears for cutting flesh and cracking bones (the carnassial teeth).

Herbivores: the incisors are sharp and are often worn down on one side to give a chisel-like edge. The incisors and canines are often missing on the upper jaw, and in some animals the canines are missing altogether. The upper and lower molars and premolars fit against each other to provide a grinding surface.

3. Dental formulae

	I	C	P	M	*teeth*
Man	2 2	1 1	2 2	3 3	= 16 × 2 = 32
Dog	3 3	1 1	4 4	2 3	= 21 × 2 = 42
Sheep	0 3	0 1	3 4	3 3	= 17 × 2 = 34
Rabbit	2 1	0 0	3 2	3 3	= 14 × 2 = 28

Key I – incisor P – premolar
C – canine M – molar

MOLAR TOOTH

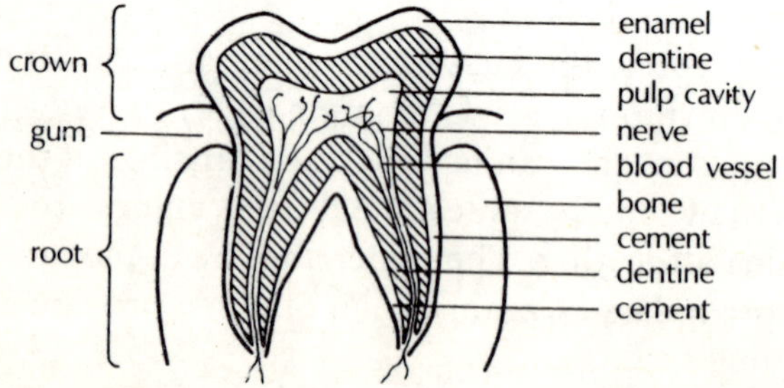

TETRAPOD
A four-footed animal, usually referring to vertebrates other than fish.

THORAX
In vertebrates it is the region of the body containing the heart and lungs. In insects it is the first three segments behind the head, and bears the legs and wings.

TISSUE
Cells forming living material of various kinds.
Examples: muscle tissue, nervous tissue.

TRACHEA
The 'wind-pipe'. A tube leading from the throat to the lungs. In insects tracheae are tubes leading to the smaller tracheoles which allow air to enter for respiration.

TYRANNOSAURUS
Giant carnivorous reptile, living about 150 million

years ago. Some weighed over 20 tons, and were about 20 feet high.

UNICELLULAR

Refers to an organism consisting of only one cell. *Examples:* amoeba, paramecium.

UREA

A nitrogen-containing compound. Poisonous nitrogen compounds formed in the breakdown of amino acids in the body are converted to urea, and are excreted in the urine via the kidneys.

UTERUS

The womb. Part of the female reproductive system. It is here that the fertilised egg is implanted, and develops as the embryo of the new individual.

VARIATION (See *Natural Selection*)

VEINS

Blood vessels carrying blood back to the heart.

Except for the pulmonary veins which carry oxygenated blood from the lungs to the left auricle, the veins carry de-oxygenated blood to the right auricle of the heart.

VERTEBRAL COLUMN
The backbone of a vertebrate.

VILLUS (*pl.* villi)
Small finger-like projections on the inner surface of the small intestine. These provide a large surface area through which products of digestion can be absorbed into the blood.

VIRUS
Micro-organisms, neither plant nor animal precisely. They are smaller than bacteria, and are able to live and multiply within the cells of animals and plants. They cause many different diseases.

VITAMINS
Chemicals required by animals in small quantities in their diet. Their lack causes what are known as 'deficiency diseases'. *Examples:* Lack, or deficiency

of vitamin C causes scurvy, and of vitamin B1 beri-beri.

VIVIPAROUS
Describes animals whose young develop in the mother's body and not in a shelled egg.

WHITE BLOOD CELLS
Cells present in the blood in variable numbers which combat disease and infection.

YOLK
Food store present in the egg.

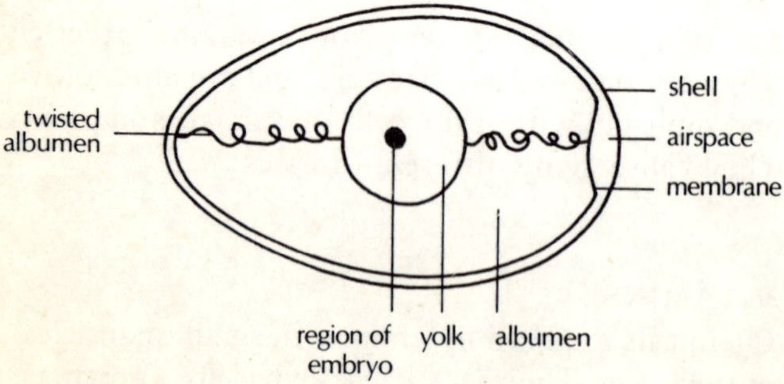

HEN'S EGG